The Shadow of David

THE SHADOW OF DAVID

Romy Erikson

COSMONAUT PHOEBUS | NEW YORK CITY

The Shadow of David 'Poems' – Copyright © 2017 by Romy Erikson
Shadow Faces 'Line Drawings' – Copyright © 2017 by Romy Erikson

All rights reserved. No part of this publication may be reproduced, distributed or transmitted in any form or by any means, without prior written permission.

Romy Erikson / Cosmonaut Phoebus
P.O. Box 98
Sparkill, N.Y / 10976

Publisher's Note: This is a work of fiction. Names, characters, places, and incidents are a product of the author's imagination. Locales and public names are sometimes used for atmospheric purposes. Any resemblance to actual people, living or dead, or to businesses, companies, events, institutions, or locales is completely coincidental.

Designed and typeset by Oliver Preston

The Shadow of David/ Romy Erikson – 1st ed.

This book is dedicated to my daughters Darcy and Gala.

We're born alone, we live alone, we die alone. Only through our love and friendship can we create the illusion for the moment that we're not alone.

— ORSON WELLES

CONTENTS

Introduction   XI

On Paradise Lies

Shadow to Shadow	3
No Other Story	5
A Note for David	7
The Unborn	10
Twenty Three	11
Dress for Depression	13
Dead Man's Sun	14
Return	16
Wallpaper	19
Butterflies	21
Passion	23
God	26

Absolute Nothings

Forgotten	31
Skyland	33
Desire	35
Wonder	36
David	37
King	40
Stranger	43

Open Window

Hope	47
Carnal	48
The Devil's Halo (1)	51
The Devil's Halo (2)	52
The Devil's Halo (3)	53
The Moonlit Room	54
Me to Myself	57
The Dog	59
The Portrait	60
The Need	62
Shibo	63
The Knife Men	65
The Other Odin	66

Empty Homes

The End of Innocence	71
The Mirror	72
Poetic Drafts	73
On the Bridge	75
Human	76
The Lone Wolf	77
Sluts on Fire	78
Sixteen Years	79

New Ending

Mourning	83
Slice of Me	84
Husband	86
Cavemen	88
Atomic Aliens	91
Space Crows	95
The Mad Blues	97
The Crazy Horse	98
The End	99
Saint	100
Secret Waters	102

Introduction

This poetic collection began in 2002 after attempts to complete a novel titled Normal Lives failed due to my lack of experience as a writer, and unsettling occurrences beyond my control that affected my ability to focus. Poetry has always been my preferred method of therapy when I feel unable to cope, for it draws on the journey without judging it. I allowed my heart and my mind to go wherever it wanted to take me, and it always went to a place of love and understanding.

David and his shadows slammed doors repeatedly in my Manhattan building in groups of one, two, three, four, five and six loud bangs until ten every night, so between the hours of ten and seven in the morning, I sat in the kitchen table with my coffee cups lined up and I wrote poetry knowing it was going to get impossibly noisy again during the day.

That hell found building in midtown Manhattan and its endless amount of door slamming inspired my relationship with a fictitious demon called David, and his imaginary shadows. New to America and to New York, I imagined then that a superpower or a celebrity wanted to meet me, although I wasn't sure that I wanted him. Fame and power were irresistible illusions, door banging and strangers stalking me were not. My suspicions were many years later discovered to be unromantic, but that is not what my poetry is about, for on these pages I abide only to my work that absorbs both my suave or cruel experiences and expresses the things that they inspire.

Having a true obsession for great love stories, I waited patiently between the years of 2002 and 2006 for the noise to end and for this mysterious door banger to introduce himself to me. I loved my so called David until my body and my mind gave up on me although my spirit never surrendered the hope that David was some sort of diabolical angel in disguise for his shadows took me on the strangest journey inside of me. I appreciated receiving lots of door banging attention for it inspired The Shadow of David, Master, The Butterflies and other works. It was evil attention, but it was much needed attention!

I sincerely apologize for the pain that decorates my first poetry collection, to such a horrifying excess, that I cannot help but laugh about it in the end. The era of David and his shadows were to me about reexperiencing loss and remembering the dead. David as a demon performer, David as the devil's shadow, David as a death memory. In the beginning, I wanted the lies that David showed me about our future to be different, but they were no different from my past burdens. He mirrored them, as shadows do best. I closed my eyes to evil, turned my face away, and allowed David to destroy me, for he had nothing else to offer. The world has many demons and its shadows, they come in forms of wars, technology, knowledge, words, pictures, people, events and other demons. I take responsibility for not being able to escape, a self-defining hell that I helped build, and later found impossible to cease.

Today, I respect my naïve expectations at that time, my insistence in inventing my own twisted version of an American Dream, and the existence of the fictitious shadows like those I fabricated of David, because they helped me outlive my fears; and those fears were, in most past, about having a real life. I later found that the seeds of birth, growth and love were not a terrifying experience to evade. When I overcame my fear of reality, death and other similar nauseas, I started finally finding the humor in the self-aggrandizing drama I had imprisoned myself too.

The end sometimes, if not always, is a chance to make a new beginning. And after my heart died in the arms of a door slamming David, I found renewed strength in every breath of air and laughter. I have forgiven David and his shadows, and most importantly, I have forgiven my shadow for not seeing the light that illuminates us all.

Romy Erikson

On Paradise Lies

SHADOW TO SHADOW

The night is blue
The rain is black
The sun is white
The ocean is green
The sand is gold
The moon is asleep, and it all happens at once.

The orange butterflies fly around the white sun, and flick sunsets on my eyes.
The rocks are diamonds that reflect to the sun, a thousand times white.
The gray trees are taller than earth, and breeze the starry grayer universe.
The skin that covers my shadow is yellow, from the gold dust the wind blew.
The children play and laugh with fate's spheres, that fly high for a very long time.
Their eyes are red beams that reflect the hearts, in their heads just like yours
      and mine.
And I must walk, I must keep on walking, I must never stop climbing this shore
      for you.

The night is blue and it sometimes whistles.
The rain is black and it sometimes screams.
The sun is white and it sometimes pretends.
The ocean is green and it sometimes moans.
The sand is gold and it sometimes loves.
The moon is asleep and it sometimes observes.
It happens only sometimes, we also walk past silences.

Since I've known you, bees pose honey on my curls.
Since I've known you, baby turtles hitch on my toes.
Since I've known you, purple children follow my paths.
Since I've known you, grey ants on trees screen my thoughts.
Since I've known you, green oceans hammer poems on my footsteps.
Since I've known you, black rain greases a gun with my fears.
I panic to lose you and I panic to have you but heaven flies on hell's echoes.

You teach me so much with your strange shadow, that will not allow me
      to stop dreaming.
You love me so dearly with your strange shadow, that will not allow me

    to stop sacrificing.
You silence me so painfully with your strange shadow, that will not allow me
    to stop dying.

My life is this secret since I think you love me but tell me why do you own me?
My days sacrifice the moon's patience, when my disgrace seems your grace.
My shadow could also lie for planets could evaporate, or maybe deteriorate.
My tears are pale beige wounds from the kisses of your snakes, in love?

I must walk, I must keep walking, I must never stop climbing this shore for you.
Children with purple skin play, run, race, raise, rest, and return every color to you.
Our red beam eyes for the hearts in our heads map a planet about you.

The night is blue and it sometimes whistles.
The rain is black and it sometimes screams.
The sun is white and it sometimes pretends.
The ocean is green and it sometimes moans.
The sand is gold and it sometimes loves.
The moon is asleep and it sometimes observes.
It happens only sometimes, we also walk past silences.

From shadow to shadow,
I must never stop walking,
On paradise lies, sometimes so low.

NO OTHER STORY

I have no other story
I have no other glory
I have no other memory

Poor, cheap, out of style
Borrow cash and go a mile
Despise the story I call mine

I have nothing from you
I know nothing about you
I hate you and you and you!

The Shadow is more than human
The Shadow is less than a man
The Shadow rules Manhattan

Powerful, playful, deceitful
Maybe you're so beautiful
Now you're f* beep awful

Heidi wrote my number on a dollar
Quiet nineteen ninety nine, winter
December, I no longer remember

You called and called
Ideas of you started
In the men I dated

You sent me meat
You know, men to eat
My reality you did cheat

Cellphone, cyber
Home wired, stalker
Poisoned water

Who is this?
Silences
Loneliness?

I love you, move away
I hate you, stay away
I want you, far away

A NOTE FOR DAVID

In the end,
seven years gone dead
in a song
for each leg
that walks,
just walks.

Everywhere lover
you're lovelier.

In the end
seven years old
look left,
and right.

Surrender then
on and on amen.

Wiser but older
Neither stronger
nor weaker.

Dreams now sleep
so deep
inside silence,
indifferent solitude.

Go then
seven.

Good fortune love,
remember me,
or something,
anything
seems fine.

You were nice.
Five or six:
Yeah just sex,
in the end,
to hold,
to imagine.

Everyday!

I say you
age
by my side.

Lately
you gray
wolf.

Just stuff,
details.

Bite my nails,
imagine,
but all's fine.

In the end
only you stand
in the wild
seas.

I mean sees
possible
to dream
of a stream
that leads
familiar heads.

Funnier strangers
David?
Never David.

In the end
roses to send:
To hell
with a bell.

Who cares
for scares.

Except,
except
when you
weren't
you.

Now,
even now.

After seven
only seven
repeat again
repeat
over and over
push further.

Some hope;
any little one
and live on
walk on
sleep in
your smile.

UNBORN

I don't mean anything by these words
for I was never born from them.

They found me waiting for their swords
for they hailed down on me.

Opened my arms to be hit by seven of God,
ran away to be found by the Devil's iron one.

Yelled about something lost
a piece of faith that was left.

I am the unborn fate,
it must be why my heart's full of hate.

Unable to find a reason that saves me on time,
dwell about silence without a note to anyone.

I let my heart go its own way,
sometimes I dance the curse away.

Because every night feels closer to the last,
it doesn't matter if swords rain down or not.

They're in my brain causing me pain,
piercing my chest with sin.

Who cares about what I do,
or feel when the answer is No.

Try to forget the unborn is me,
and throw my life a dime.

TWENTY-THREE

Every day
Impatient eternity
Impotency
Powerful and lively

Every day
Rolling rock skies
Too many lies
Smoking girly

Every day
Satisfy somebody
Maybe lonely
Drunkenly till merry

Every day
Fast-forward carpeting
Future binding
Over viewing the silly city

At night
Anxiously ready
Vrooming away
Anyone at sight

Daylight
Soaking on smiles
Pleasure and adores
Connect with any socket

At twenty-three
Eat words for free
And free see all
Including the suicide wall

At twenty-three

Worker bee philosophy
Now pee eternally
Intoxicated me

Every day, every day
Repeat, repeat yesterday
Dream, nightmare, dream
Again, again free me

Powerful twenty-three
Clowns me
Sadly smile
At any but only me.

DRESS FOR DEPRESSION

Sleeps abandoned on the bare mattress
Seeks punishment with bitter rawness
Blessed the closed eyes that angels kiss
Feels the strangeness of each existence
Harbors ghosts of lovers in their eclipse
Skin deep latex woes on nobody's bride
This female is raw sex altogether.

DEAD MAN'S SUN

dedicated to Cesar

I see a dead man walk closer to me,
His smile is ageless, but seems now hollow.
Clouds above our heads are intensely yellow,
But the sky's a scissor cut collage of mine.

I see the dead man's numb eyes are brown,
Summer shades inside. He wanders in there,
Where a girl calls his name from the shore,
Both lost. His head turns with no intention.

I see a dead man's legs limp him on.
He wears a black suit. But he's blind to it.
White roads walk his feet. Fear's in his night,
Painful without stars, or moon, or horizon.

I see a dead man's bruised face in chaos.
His sons exit memories like freed runways,
His wife's smiles are mere halo rays,
A supersonic bike flies into silver steel.

I see the dead man's fingers that my lips kiss,
Into the eternal adore that bounds us timeless.
Sunbathe under many lights and wait sickless,
my lil' loves die when one from there sinks.

I see a dead man pass along indifferent to me,
We are bluntly forbidden outside our mind.
Lifeless spits, wounds a poem, frames on wood.
Leaves like sundown, that's all that I hate.

I see the dead man's laughter is an earthquake.
Nobody to blame. No longer in the mood to dance,
This tiring second peels his skin like an orange,
Plucks bones as if feathers: With roots and its trees.

Death comes and goes, leaves only one less,
That's the only confusion. Kind of funny, I guess.
Hopes good-bye. I see a man whose love was sin,
Lying under a dead man's sun: My yellow new moon.

RETURN

dedicated to Cesar

Return, don't leave me with the dead
Then, you must love me instead

Man and muse, run from mourn
Listen to the echoes in my garden

A shadow fiend with no name
Sings, since you, the old same

Unaware he lives off your heat
Palled pink roses spring your seat

Your garden's very picturesque
My hunger's always grotesque

Again, spring's infatuation blossoms
Against oak trees filled with thorns

You're my golden child's engineer
Me too, our soul's rebel lovegineer

Forever a friend without a question
Rain down under cupid's direction

Six feet tall grass made of tears
Rests far from our flesh's errors

My kisses cry along with my blood
Dead feels you are now good

Crystallized monument in the sky
As ceilings in treasure caves, obey

Return, don't leave me with the dead
Then, you must love me instead

Sin Likes Sugar, Honey it's me Purple!
That never anywhere kind of turtle

An ancient marble Queen lays to rest
Her right hand is on her shy left breast
She's cold and warm and silent

Dreams of her faraway soul mate
Your garden, our cemetery, my life
Come again you are my real safe

Where tulips are worse than poison
Perverse like tongues, hurting from within

Carnivorous emotions on petal guitars
Unlike our Let's Get Bored in little rivers

Clouds accuse me of being Purple Pink Floyd
But it's a fugitive rose with a superstar mood

Write on a tree made with my skin
End exhausted in The Nicest Smile Inn

You are a master of love-write method
A Ninja motorcycle flies you numbed

Only the bed sleeps in this Hopeless Room
You remove your glasses in your doom

Somber without, you look happier with them
Funny, a smiling mask or no smiling glum

That Romeo expression simply grins
A ghost's laughter supersedes shadows

You stretch your arms for my embrace
Weird fulfillments enjoy only a stage

Hold me real hard in this blind wish
Memory feathers and farewells hush

Slide me to my knees with nostalgia
Ride on to rescue a woman's ninja

Your wild side never burns anybody
This twin ghost flowers my whole body

Truths feel suave from your voice
A rush of autumn leaves cuts you free

From me that screams at the exit: Faith
God kills a good man, and it tastes like filth

Time wraps dust on the last pink roses
This garden of wishes softly fades

Shows your girl in a sleepless valley
Says madly sad she loved you terribly

We bow down to your mountain's illusion
The hurt of your departure feels unknown

That nice thing in you that cannot stay later
Silks of our private dreams sink underwater

Soon it will be harder to feel the delicate truth
Death and life and love in all gardens breath

The marble Queen has no desire to return
To fate's desolation.

WALLPAPER

dedicated to Cesar

Apartment lights from another building wallpaper the window.
Bricks of lives spread like pictures of people never seen,
Few as dark as ghosts; empty spaces that they sleep in.

Cover my lips with my hands, rest on the glass' cold support.
Look upon a room with a unique green grass tinted lamp,
A lone queen size bed, with tossed blankets that somewhere fall.

Maybe over there a little girl plays with her little toys and its buttons.
Mends sorrow with grace, aware of corners without her dolls' Beep.
Someday learns to weep when impotency's unable to seal into sleep.

The shadow of a black man enters the bedroom frame, and stills my moment,
I cry while I spy, notice the slim figure is my voice; I close these inward eyes.
Mourn surrendered, with vacant rooms in my heart for merely wanderers.

A white sheet curtains my bare feet, shiver more naked underneath.
His smile plays in my mind's disbelief. He's here to never leave,
Ever since years apart return to yesterday: Rivers of my hope.

The stranger with a green wonder switches off the view to my private garden,
Falls asleep. Tonight his heart feels foreign, speaks not even some Italian,
Silences. My eyes walk about abandoned, with no answers to far fetch.

Ten fingers uphold one another in the interface of flesh's most velvet escape,
My dreams seem now heavier than this city's starlight on concrete.
Mine like mistakes, passion cloys and death clowns, the sheet wipes my face.

Spring man's gone to heaven. My mind repeats: Why do I need this good-bye?
Because, he remains my wildest tame, and so gentle with the sashay in us girls.
Stolen love mask. Smoke from my cigarette spirals into a snake. And dissolves.

A New York couple undress under the kitchen's florescent white lights,
She unbinds the black belt from his black pants. My sad night sky fucks
Me. He spreads the curtain shut. He loves only the poems I write of us.

Tears wet my face not! My intimacies are memories of Harlot's red drums,
Whoever that bodies; possesses me instead. Satire's spoof in the love mill.
I suck water that pours into my palms from the kitchen tap. My thirst is real.

He's in the moment's blood cell. Transfusions of his perfumed times instill freedom,
Missing. The window of fiction stretches blurry in the unclean window sill,
Missing. Dial numbers on the phone that ring into their similar farewell.

Today's districts on my ceiling; friends sit on motorcycles and smile for my shot,
That shines. He poses in that word unable to farther a mile in another road.
My room's darker. He lets me go. That No never hurt until now; at the end's end.

Dawn's near. Hear his bike's engine down there in the street, suddenly none.
The nightmare's only this wallpaper that cold glass inhibits me to touch,
The lover that dies like a dream awakes today. River, thank you very much.
For your crossings with mine.

BUTTERFLIES

dedicated to the children of war

In the virgin forest
A soulful sunset.

Above the deep green
Wind makes teen.

Needle pine leaves carpet
Skin layers of velvet.

Wood mosaics
Outline lilacs.

Shy of an idol's presence
And stardom's sentence.

Prisons of innocence stolen
Hangs children.

From fins of their hair
Like butterflies
Die.

Angel eye closes
On beaches of branches.

Hundred eleven suspend
On sunshine's thread.

Fallen boys heads
Broken girls necks
Like butterflies
Die.

Little shoes swing
On crops of spring.

Wild roses
Invent blues.

For the children
And their burden.

Moist grass silences
Strings of soulful chimes.

In the virgin forests
Ghosts
Of butterflies.

PASSION

The orange Triumph motorcycle resting under the shade
of the hottest Tuesday afternoon
is my greatest passion.

In my beige dusted underwear
calmly yawn and slowly rise
from the flattest rock that ironed me to summer.

Crawl like a heated lizard for my torn denims
a kamikaze top, riding boots,
and my favorite No Fear leathers.

Ignite the motorcycle beast,
rousing quiet corners in my brain,
some rooms eternally sleep in this wilderness.

Sit on my bike thinking of him
looking somberly through my sunglasses,
a snake serpentines after a hapless lost mouse.

I screech out loud: Leave her alone!
for the hunt feels unfair
in this, actually cool, four o'clock scare.

Reach for my helmet with Eagle graffiti
he flies boldly feeling fiercely angry,
and fit it all through my small head.

Take a long dirt road to get to the freeway were some cars go
north, south, east and west
to their stupid end.

See that David's girl stands darkly,
seemingly gone with the words: No Entry,
flies buzz around like wannabe vultures.

My weird jealousy tames to mellow,
a very stabilizing psychotic condition,
for excessively pleasant rides.

We put fire on the tracks of a blue Toyota,
because it's a blue Toyota
that journeys on tea without insanity.

Share memories with a strange guest,
that worms his tires into her mountain, instead of my curve
nobody holds my Triumph motorcycle in sight.

Down the straight faster than down can hit, so the wind can hustle us away
whistle a tune on a crescent hill, head towards the center of the sun
that shines eight seconds of pure sky.

Leave the mess behind with my illusion
that nobody misses me
to race onto a new cloud.

Cross a dog with beige spots that runs
with a dinosaur bone on the opposite side, but with similar thoughts.
passion's the combustion that David needs, I repeat the words:
David's another name for my motorcycle Triumph.

GOD

God is something important, like air
People find him everywhere, except my hair
The hunter of hunters has me to trail His wild side
His bullets fire mistaken, for my art to abide
God beyond the Bible is Somebody like a child
Ride faith alone from eves to exits, because I am bold
Try to know the Creator, and find a match light for an answer
Why does it make sense when He is the fate maker?
Swim His dangerous wisdom, or derange on an empty seat
Dragons promise to tail my Cypress in this impossible start
To seek him in the starry flight with my soul to unite
This stalk of desire and despair throne everywhere of home
Bore Him for hours with brain sparks caught on jaws of sharks
Love Him, like a gentleman boyfriend that invents my marks
Comfort Him; kind of smile with the good and the bad bullets
Certain Pitiful Mountain climbers breed with murderous tops
His World shares freedom with enemies, and I am not that tall
Traps of secrets in my head suspend from a flower's survival
Trust He comprehends sentimental details that row my boat away
Life is not yet a familiar shore, so He must be Father of my stray
Together, from splendid mornings to absolute nothings, together
Forever seems a delicate spice to swim on closer to my Mother
For Love happens in the blue sky, where He must watch me try to fly
Fiction rains on combats of my cries in every fierce storm, that fury
He's insistently the invisible hunter, a curse of insane faith
Seems Earth's a small stone on an I Love God plastic bag in his wisdom tooth
But quite suddenly, a strange mountain with hopeful clouds, like I'm Moses
A single thunder roars louder than Life and Death and Universe pastes
Fairy tales runaway, and I fall into the depths of the profound wind, in love
Mother has since, hid me in deer's, wolves, trees, fires, and cities.
For God's seen me.

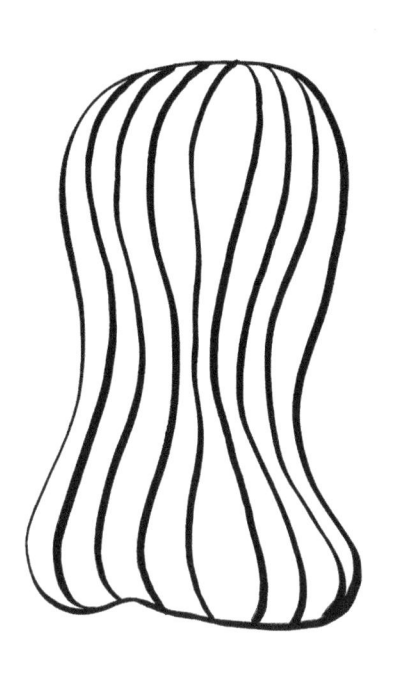

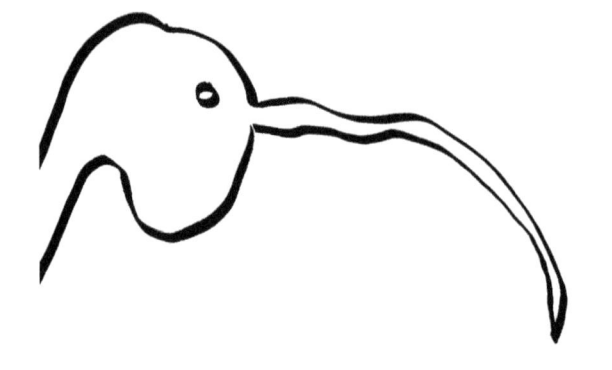

Absolute Nothings

FORGOTTEN

The two of us in a New England cottage
Fireplace and music instead of a child
Stage home bitter home, made of real wood
You watch me dance in your mind

Silence forever your pleasure to rid
It is not me you loath with fault
I feel more or less the same revenge
Sleep with me between the sheets

Clean or dirty, moods and moons cycle
Prisoners of forgotten dreams in space
But never hold in a New England cottage
Too soon for a child and many more

To discover each other inside
It's a prison in the blood cell
Quiet, slow, mellow love making
Stay there with my eyes open
Looking at another's moon.

SKYLAND

He loves not this poor little girl
Comes around as a friendly tear
Smooths the soul just like a pill
Drops casual pink on her tiny fear

Cape Cod, nineteen-eighty-one
A special sky lives in her head
Earth merely traces each pace
In-between red curtains seed

Prays for him on her knees
For a true home with no night
Father's stranger than God sees
Switches off days with his spirit

Unlove by force is painful faith
One million stabs of blue eyes
Inhale the smoke of earths ash
Skyland is real love on hell eves

Swims down the shore unable to stop
Shocked by this need to think alone
The mind bites before teeth rip
Skyland rents out tips of confidence

Home's a fly caught on a spider web
Where frogs compose nature's burps
And her shadows wear a nice red bib
The head on fire literally never ends

Cape Cod's bedrooms are emptied
The future is Skylands dirty legacy
Poor girl's footsteps are bloodied
Crying she washes floors obsessively

Unable to survive without dreams
Prohibited of particular thoughts
Fishes Poe's Conqueror of Worms
Words bury her with earthly twists

A pregnant duck figures this mess
In the morning hours before ten
Sways over screeching lil' spiders
And frees her shadowy imagination

Skyland's an afternoon sunbathe
His legs tower her pink swimsuit
Dozes under a shiny new breath
Inside the whole of his midnight

Back again into the dusk
Fear the motionless horizon
A mad heart hides in a clock
True home sans this fever

Skyland's a flame in black
Panic not this poor girl's trap
Shadows pick on wild vacancies
The head on fire runs for help
Skyland buys her pair of red shoes
Brightening the girl's tacky slop.

DESIRE

When the night falls my body swallows the dark.
Whole through the hole in the wall like a rock.
Whiny fingers bleed cold the hungry night hawk.
With a blade destroy the vein in a heartbeat deed.
What desire for freedom to sail away all my dead.

Beyond eager to anger the bad dog in good God.
Because David says human faith mends with a paper test.
But being around lumps of my blood is like berry unsweet.
Bore the escape with a fine glass of wine under my wrist.
Beat love, kick hate, bite another night and time to clean this shit.

Find this ice in the future across the mirror in a minute.
Fear the script is that moment that lives forever here.
Faint hard just like black moss on some dumb stone.
Feature lonesome in a weird film in love with me alone.
Fail again to sense anything important about this desire.

Freak the nothing in a sprint to my bed to hide David more.
Fight the man that broke my wings to leave me bare.
Fall again and again fall and fall again without a blade.
White sheets with too much pain is like trashing rain for a blue.
Finally wail my head into David's pillow which is now mine.

(Whatever desire whatever feeling to just calm me.)
(Whine, help me help me help me please.)
(Whisper, okay to whatever desire.)
(Help me!)

WONDER

I wonder if every thought is born wrong
Why does my life seem permanently frail?
Obsess about my chances diminishing away
My bulb of light is too old for somewhere
Roads without true friends except this heat
A bed that tears nest and knows just that
Something unforgivably lost is everywhere
Searching for a hand without a doubt, please
Wonder in much less than perfection really
A piece of normal life and a daily certainty
Little cubes of cherry sweets taste all right
Maybe my voice shouldn't sound faraway
Silence should cease to drill on imagination
Nothing to pray for but a Smoke It dream
Heaven has only skies for the real people
Watching every hunger that is only mine
Destiny perhaps I still fear always more
Wondering in the mistaken right turn
Last cup of illusions tastes like dirt water
Forever more wonder even about my fleas
Their lifestyles and their opinions too
I am gigantically significant but unloved
There's also a reason to marry a worm
Who is devoured by a sensual horror woman
Me on the last stop without plans
Only wonder.

DAVID

dedicated to musician David Sylvian

To live in melodies is the wildest thing
Soundless contingencies steal the being
To breathe in words is the vilest thing
Morning triumphs with David's song.

Outside the hawk-dogs fly to bark me inside
In a cage for foxes cries a bird from paradise
Live in a forbidden corner without pleasure
Feel David cleanse me with gentle hope

At the doors of heaven the day is long with defeat
Fear my wounds like the knife is actually my heart
Guess all's necessary to breed giants out of seconds
That run away with us in them and leave behind traps

David is the fallen coin from a beggars tip
Joy in the fire swing ride to appease the sip
For I am in love with the hue of a night star
Wear music like an umbrella to feel love fair

In the end there's only art to bury everything
And just nothing but nothing to do about anything
Love won't escape anymore: Hell Angels surrender
Fly lost in the shelter of his possible future lover

His infernal spaceship lives longer than a killer drug
Light cigarettes for death to smoke in my tight cling
White clouds and black winds hold us endlessly strong
We are the tall cliffs that blue oceans must wrong

David's voice casts me deeper into the madness
The couple in love motion our story to his drums
The blue phoenix finds me instead in sicker slums
His guitar ropes me deeper into our shadows

In deep sleep most of the day as well
David's piano on my feelings drill
Loneliness swings down the religious cliff
Hold tight to a stone in my palm to throw at Disbelief

The weakened shore wraps my feet with bound mud
Blue curtains flare over dunes faraway in the end
Run barefoot on the canvas of a once upon a time sea
Scream furiously for the blue sky promises to cease.

KING

David is King of my kink and my blue
My muse is true to the most wicked lie
Loves me with a certain kind of blood dye.

Every day I feel a very teeny bit better, or worse
The whole of me lives locked in our lovely dark universe
We share a hellhole of kingdoms, or somewhere close.

King David slams the door penetrating my space
Your Majesty shatters the walls slapping my face
Excellency pulls me into a hole that we call home.

Touch my naked skin much more bare than I dare
David has the preferable face in this improved disgrace
Tortured but apparently okay by an exquisite muse.

Love me King with my legs open in three
Caned woman in red tomato juice: Blood, Rush, Bite
Suffocate: Deathless and out of air! I suffer comrade.

Whenever I want his Shadow, I know Hell is Here
David will severely crown my fucked brain with a heart core
It won't be a tragic hour for his whore, although no more!
Much more please.

STRANGER

Let me rest by my tomb brother
I am tomorrow's complete stranger
Carry your sunshine from hell further
With a lover, or some sister, whichever
I am yesterday's forgotten daughter
Be no more my love miner.

Let me stay by us here together
Where hope sleeps under the vile weather
Understand I am today's beaten thunder
Loud things to sometimes remember
Although torn away memories are heavier
Be no more my hate digger.

Let me spread some dust from my tears
Your flowers bloom on the cuts of my flesh
A new love towers us, but mine you continue to crash
Less than human is the portrait of me now to wash
Cry my soul dry, and try man, try really try, to win my fears
Be not even my cadaver.

Let me rest now by the tomb ugly brother
I am this afternoon, stranger than a dead singer
Whatever more details do not awake this still hour
The midnight moon is too bright to roll me down like murder
Love lives eternally in my innocence that these deserts sour
Take the last picture of me and go father.

I am just a stranger by now.

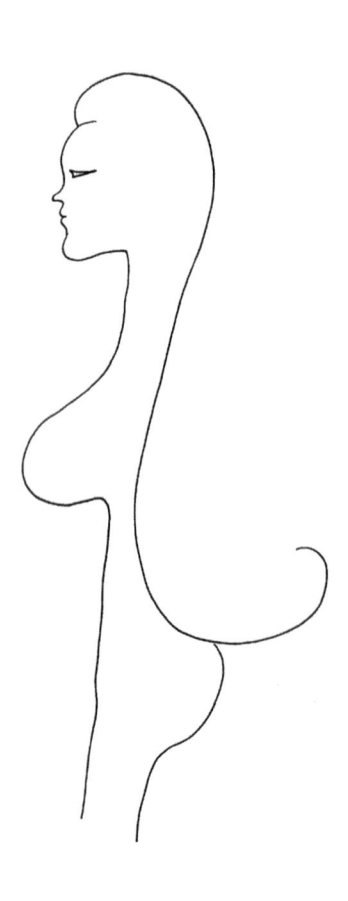

Open Window

HOPE

A bar down the street rules my hope with noises of clasping bottles of beer
A window chooses to picture freedom is not far away from here
A silver curtain opens to the moon's unfaltering beauty to save me of a tear
A tragic story preys on my ring finger that vows sorrow in my prayer
A man's kiss on my lazy hot cheek rests close to my lip for a whisper
A black dress unbuttons my blood in the wilderness of each night lonelier
A friend with blonde moist hair stabs his body trapping me in my lair
A few steps from the sound of a telephone and a black leather armchair
A moan from inside of a single white hall blows alive yet another intruder
A lip bites through another raw act that makes a flower vase spill its water
A throb of his cock fulfills the lust for our real sex that could once more be my frail liar
A cat in heat that lives on an oak tree shouts louder than fists of falling bottles of beer
A fine tongue burns against the sheets of trapped hope that I wish to power
A ghost's thread suspends a black spider from a swinging bulb
Silver fog moves astray from my open window.

CARNAL

You can never predict when the sexual man
turns his eyes light or exactly when you awake late
eternally baby, drunk.

With insatiable more, sheets sink beneath pools sleep
down on resemblance, passion for the slip,
swims any scene.

Freedom Please! Never sugar!
Watch your face thinner and bitter,
because that bird flew long ago.

Boiling oceans you war
what no God owns
the sexual purr.

Always excited, hope in pussy sown,
always frustrated,
Jesus your frown.

Thinking you free?
Every rejection jungle elevator, alone and sore
dream to pair as if he were a freak weasel face.

Quixote loved a mill, road to madden
find him or else woman ghost,
searching everywhere for a gift.

Then a fat frown and lots of make-up
smile even sown,
bore the up with repetition.

That now cloud has a longer chain,
bark out loud, make a movie star,
feel all impotencies for he doesn't purr.

Just salts the sea which you boil,
then can't swim, live to pay the bill
of the heaviest dream.

Now jobless fucking mirrors, and dandruff mess
Eternally repair mechanics of lust,
making love to a prayer, wanting bad to reset.

Sweeten walls and directly to the tongue
they also have bills, Billy you mortgage
cleaned-you-out-too.

Vampire you now go idiot, no howling
suck your own blood and satiate me,
every horny mood paper to shame.

Nobody cares you are now mad. Yes, cow yes!
drink all that is bad, make it worse to forget
eat a magazine or make a bet.

Adapt all to sex
play Shadow # Six
Peter may last it seems.

Satiate smiley away to Hollywood
Kings of Dildos and queens of Reflection, climax on Zeros'
imagination always pays back, see men in black, love that wood.

Sexual man, yes
made you madden, yes
you realize late, tattooed forever.

Like a dog,
cloud lover,
chain a song…

Whistle along then bang, never sang,
jobless gong go with Peter, nothing gets eviler
imagine soccer, always in character.

THE DEVIL'S HALO (1)

Mystic prisons call out our names with a sense of urgency
There's a darkening horizon where we can hide immediately
Traumatic images of unprevented enemies set the night
And we must crawl the familiar ground full of deceit
Fingers root into Earth in search of a burning death in my mind
My love's home is torn away by the pain in my blood
Finally hit Nowhere Wall that true faith pitches of black
Sculpt my real soul with my cheeks that want him back
The end will be eternally tomorrow that sunglasses every day
Death is a friendlier version than what people say
Shrink to the cell to swim in every wound's pool
Red cold muck clings to my shivers until stern with all
Yell unexpectedly for my mama to please water my mouth
The Devil's halo lingers on from pore to pore; a shark tooth in each
No reply except earthquakes and this share of nothing; consoles
Surrender and obey fate; and every lover that me hates
Electric shocks vein across the tender memories of kisses
Burst into nervous laughter wondering who's my master
Finally a greater lust for this deeper than human fighter
Truth or trick but we must drill out all this suffering at once
Costs only ten pounds and a wick bit of flesh to be free
From mystic prisons that must stop calling out our names

THE DEVIL'S HALO (2)

Tiptoe on delicate beings within whose loudest screech let me begin
Choose one amongst millions of tears; the heaviest of tonight's chain
There's a close enough black door on the background entitled: Exit Death
Grab onto this desire of him as if the image is my key to health
Nails scratch the sharp pores that do not trust blindly in us
The flesh strikes back with infected old scars full of pus
Intoxicate love on the self-loath cross road to drop dead
Starve the satanic oxygen in my brain to be whole with the devils head
At last a sincere everlasting versicle: our kisses rouse impossible roofs
Years trying to understand why love slammed all doors
Deaf God, bearing demon that feels the stink of our rotting feet
Love kisses me goodnight and goodbye; his tongue stabs my throat
Can't mend nor sow with the hottest blow this lone abandonment
Sluggishly die unable to uncurl my spine to weakly protect the past
The Devil snatches fifteen pounds without caring to chew the damned
Punches my lungs so I take breathing cuts for crying beyond his shield
I am possessed by the father that drank most of my soul with his bloody wine
Feel much in this last night on earth for this is the most intimacy I've held in my life
The flesh battles our demons alone spitting the agony but the end never arrives
Exit Death is the impossible key to find amongst the teeth of my pores
A bottled body of blood that flushes like piss from many holes
The Devil doesn't wish us to end but just to hang from his knives
Our insomniac worry becomes insane in Nowhere's Wall
The Devil huskily sings: Perhaps he never kissed you at all!

THE DEVIL'S HALO (3)

He never expressed any desire to kiss my cheeks
The Devil sucks on tonight's longest tear to salt his steaks
At last an immutable bone collection lies as silent as eternity
Inch by inch memories wrinkle colors off any devoured story
Distant sirens of ambulances howl to frightened away screams of dreams
Childlike eyeballs observe carefully these still hungry demons
Roll out of stabbing knives somewhat bored
Walk in circles dragging my stiff toes curled
The floor is hot as rock on fire which is interesting
My shut up ugly skeleton or clown feels something exciting
Certainly, more present now than having a ghost lover
Never been any realer, any thinner; never felt better
Whatever day of week or moths name; it's me for real
Stalks of acidy odors founded a diva's soul!
But kind of late arrives this halo of might to unwind mistakes
The Devil pities my fallen skull and returns it to the puzzles
This woman rows left and right to hint a dance
Sadly, he must hold me tight from slipping down this chance
His shoulders pillow my head crushed together for more sin
We waltz in silence awkwardly united without much pain
This song is our life from which it is impossible to part
An arduous walk from this mess waits to start
I am nothing to agree or disagree; I am free experience
Unroot my fingers from Earth although the night comes with me
The Devil mumbles along: He hates you like I do
Smile and humbly bow: Seems like that will do, let's go.

THE MOONLIT ROOM

A silent affair at an address unknown
Loom nine Shadows from Nine moons
Walk downstairs with unclear passages
Like an excited child inhale the cold air
Mystery plays one of my favorite games
Hurry to feel nine Eagles inside nine Wolves
Dogs bark against gates built for their souls
The starry sky glows on my green eyes
The door with no street number is open
Undress my Body at the carpeted entrance
White lights guide my Spirit along space
Walk quickly to the last door without fear
Enter a moonlit room with nine windows
Nine Shadows with nine white stares await
To each walk expecting true love in return
One caresses only my hair until I feel mad
One kisses my face but separates our body
One touches my skin with his handsome lips
One ignores my affection until I'm defeated
One takes my hand and rubs it on his sex
One bites my neck and sucks my blood
One carries me in his arms to the next one
One lays me down in bed to make love to all
One cleans my sex with his Shadow tongue
Silence lives eternally in our brief intimacy
The nine Shadow men are my moonlit room
Every yearning wonders from one to the other
Earth has only One moon to dream on
My secrets sleep with me every night
Dream about a world that might come
His Shadow is not enough for me to love
I take his moon for mine until the end of time
In the privacy of a kiss I begin all over again
To feel the One inside his skin through nine Loves.

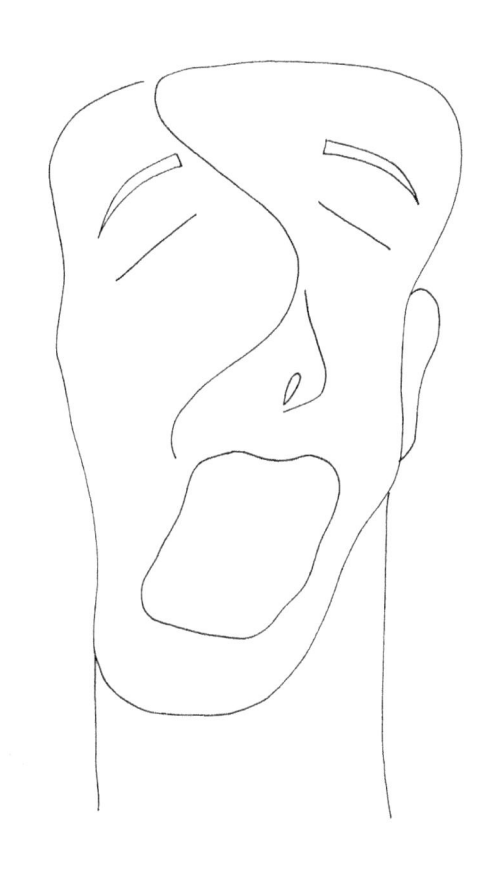

ME TO MYSELF

Thank you very much Thief
Introducing Me to Myself.
Aspire an abstract manhood
Fattening as male junk food.
Our world should never exist
Love really is fascinating shit.
A name will build you a street
And design me a precise hat.
Reality must be made of stones
You see wrongs in my bones.
Cried hard for that Billy boy
An utter stranger to this silly.
You style my bloody emotions
And dress my body of moans.
Guess there's no true love to tell
Thanks for the money from hell.
An expression satirizes my stare
Your note says: Hang In There!
Be cruel instead to your mother
I refuse to be your tame tiger.
Now possess a world of fiction
Paid with a spoon of my blood.
Give it all to you to fix that cold
For your Shadow to make bold.
Nothing left except Me to Myself
That's now her dearest Thief.
Shadows love us both with lies
Nowadays nobody except skies.
Struggle along attempts to story
Pathetic love without the boy.
Trash on my honorable head
My strange desires to mend.
Picture my fate in this sadness
A selfie of injured madness.
Thank you very much beef

You set me free of Myself
Slam objects out of the way
Unable to now store you away.
This cannot be just nothing
You're in my skin burning.
Made an insane bet on paper
Twelve years are no stranger.
The pen writes to somebody
The dice indicate nobody.
Enter the game for you alone
Pick me up and take me home.
No Me to Myself as excuse
Your Shadow marries mine.
Hello again man of matter
More than data to master.
Not kneeling before photos
Sick of inventing my mottos.
Spirit and Shadow are Me
Your heart on my tongue.
Beg you to payback in kind
My crimson lips do not mind.
Me to Myself: My own Thief.
Many lies and follies still to free.

THE DOG

I am a Dog.

Love my master's Socks.

Except if he whistles,
Or barks.

Curl my tail in,
My ears wither.

Exit through a pin,
Running from winter.

It is best to not think,
Arrogance bulls men.

Many masters sink,
Many more to hem.

Around him I crawl,
I whimper and I moan.

Sympathy is no shawl,
Truly adore no mean.

THE PORTRAIT

The one I love to hate
A demon designed by God
In a family portrait of Shadows
He looks mutably indifferent
The one from my deliriums
Makes me uncomfortable
The portrait of love
Dangerously inspires
Sculptured on fine stone
His presence is untouchable
Once upon a scared boy
Who wanted to lead
No innocent blue eyes
His mouth is a straight line
Were handsome lips crown
Blond short side swept hair
A strict thin expression
He looks undefeatable
Destined to protect faith
From unconfident humans
Wonder how would it feel
To touch his handsome portrait
His skin and that so on attitude
Now he's kicked me out a few times
Placed me with the dead folders
Sent me one-on-one hitmen
Religion really excites me
Masturbation is barred
Except he is my muse
My platonic thing
He looks human
With an alien core
Out to kill our souls
A chance to provoke him
Can never be declined

His only weakness
Now tea with a portrait
Of a Shadow of God.

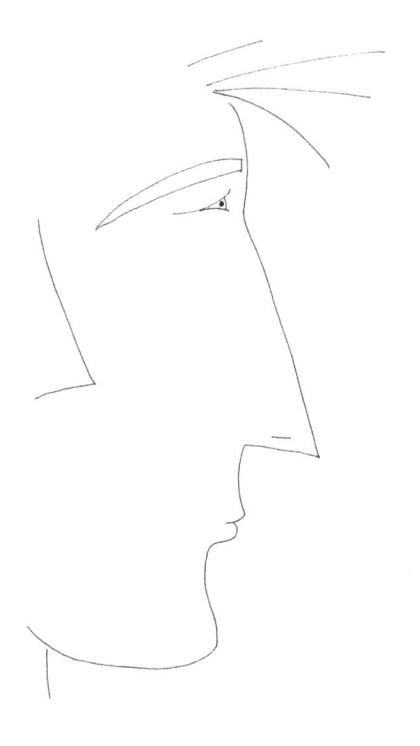

THE NEED

Greater than an avenue with traffic to heaven
An urge that grows everywhere like green grass
Forgets yet also forges tomorrow's sunny mountain
Written words with me fall asleep on sea shores
Universes and stars frustratingly unfound here
Unable to either stop or find will elsewhere
And give away to myself as if color hungry
In the rainbow I see waves of paper auras.

SHIBO

In the chaos give birth to a memory of tender love
A child sees finally the morning's sunrise in the horizon
Runs alone to the barn with a dear dream about to fail
His bells sound on familiar green paddocked grounds
Vapors from the cold are very sweet reminiscences
She calls out Shibo with her arms stretched out
The goat's indifference is an acknowledgement
Slaughtered by grandfather that was ignorant
With no more fear for the girl that rides on
Black Beauty could be a wild goat actually
Five hard jumps and down without fury
Shibo lifts her with a nod of his two horns
There's nothing better to do after breakfast
Shibo defends any attempt to ride together
Barn world of secrets fulfill a child's boredom
Ceased by death the day granddaddy got a horse
He fought the men with his two noble horns: Shibo
"Oh come with me you black ugly goat of no good"
Her giggles followed him instead into the woods
Shibo she calls out after thirty long years
They walk side by side into the vapors
Black Beauty was her goat

THE KNIFE MEN

The Knife Men arrived at her grandfather's farm
In their old horror-stricken gray truck
She ran into narrow wood paths never looking back
Down a dry river track in a valley today forgotten
The sound of that engine heart drums in her ears
A dozen pair of eyes close-in the delirious tragedy
Their chilling fading voices after seven swift strikes
Men with knives exclusively for flesh and its soul
And ropes with mastered knots for The End
She has no fairy wings to fly the lambs away
Grabs onto her dress urging for a miracle
God breeds monsters with human heads
There are no heroes except in far away lands
The pretty landscape can't hide another tragedy
Throws stones at nowhere in the distance
Smells their flesh in the crippled wind
By the murderers of her butterflies
Her little darlings are ripped apart in pain
People must eat to feed their body's waste
Four men and her granddaddy make terrible enemies
Something in their drunken lust for food sickens
Callous hands with knots for joints holding knives
There's spat blood everywhere but no butterfly color
Men shake hands with stained smiles of death
They leave in an old horror-stricken gray truck
Butterfly souls never understand their peace.

THE OTHER ODIN

One minute of Earth's life
Five thousand human years
Ten thousand miles from here
Scans across millions of lives
Sees our black colorless world
We're the curse of giant Odin
From his sky, eternal sand-rain
Spreads long descended fears
Uninterested by any cause
Except your private sorrow
Rewinds or forward's an era
To the moment of infortune
He is ahead of every enemy
Unmoved by your noble trade
Detached from even a touch
And faith or a minute search
Sees you only when you scream
Unfurs you alive for the fire
Against the frozen breeze of demise
For you need more than death
Observes you naked
As you lay at his feet
Steps on you to eat you
Abandoned by every God
Odin's the giant beast
For those scared of life
Shivering to your own grueling cries
Odin turns away with lost interest
The fire and the black smoke burn
Emptiness ends the pain.

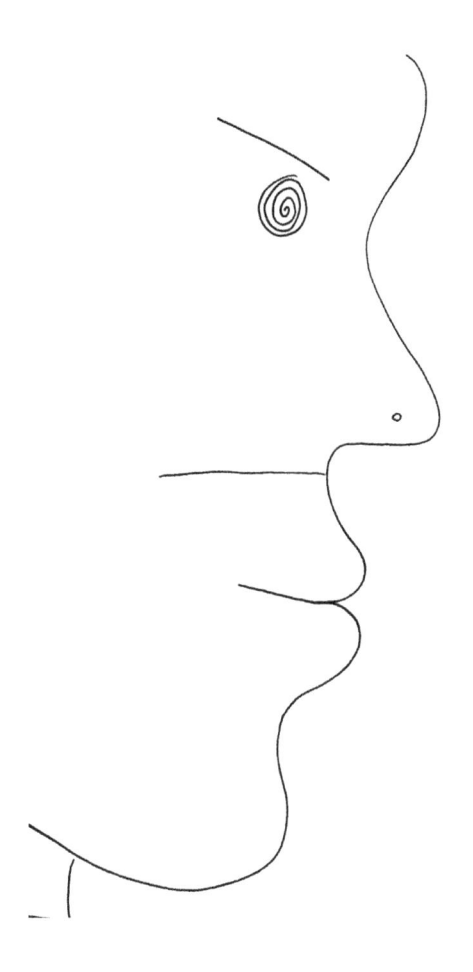

Empty Homes

THE END OF INNOCENCE

It was a cloudy and gray winter day outside
Her innocence whispered: Until Someday
Across the window, winds tunnel the trees
Just another world beyond books to travel
Rain falls shyly from this uncharacterized sky
Love's duel with Nature is a dare game they play
Heavy unromantic rain pour down her curls
She stares uninterested at the darkening horizon
Drumming of a powerful thunderstorm rises faith
Walks idly back home with dreams of this Shadow
Unknowing the end of her innocence is tomorrow
For he steals because he believes time is a fallacy
Her life freezes with pain for fifteen years
Strong winds flew her far away from herself
Pine scents at their peak slay her innocence
A lonely urge to share the afternoon with him
Innocence glows, then fades into inner beauty
These feelings are fertile in empty homes
Never gave her a choice, she never had a choice
Relationships aren't about Love, but about Nature
Wilderness of a Shadow is as forceful as a cyclone
A giant that leaves no childhood memory alive
She hates him, and runs away until someday
Little Girl in Love.

THE MIRROR

The room is painted with multiple colors
Splashed green for trees, brown for rocks
Pink for girls, blue for boys, gray for mirrors
The artist's creativity must always proliferate
The heart is the red hot sponge exaggerated
There is a painted window with a black sky
The artist and her artist heart mirror this room
A soundless silence dream was an airborne train
That led her from motion to emotion to stop
Best poet in the whole of the deserted moon
In the coldest evening of a freezing winter too
She warms her hopes on a toaster that thinks
It's really a fountain of fresh water to carry
Gets hammered down with no time to know
She moves into the pink color just for girls
Where there are blue rivers with no fish alive.

POETIC DRAFTS

More healing than to cause a toothache
The ultimate solution to deafen a heart
Or bite the tongue to change a thought
Poetic drafts bring upon a tender smile
Bits of truths and needs start to unwind
As a breeze upon curtains that blind
The inner calls that echo into a sound
It's the busiest feeling made into a song
None more important word than the next
I really hope my voice never wrinkles
With the light that a poem needs to survive
I must strengthen the message of love
In this struggle of a day by day line
Upon pages of strange discoveries
When that worry becomes a brown box
Of gifts that I never wanted to open
But this black pen draws on things
That are more captivating, magical
The farm air tastes of mother's milk
The little lamb remembers not its death
Sometimes it is hard to forget the feeling
The quiet sadness of a child who lost a friend
Grandfather killed her lamb because she limped
A black and white creature especially sweet
Something important to nurse but no longer there
Just a poem for someday to hold tight.

ON THE BRIDGE

dedicated to my sister

Open my arms to jump
Hair caught in the wind
Gales strike many blows
Drop down a heavy dream
To the open mouth of water
Through the horn of a unicorn
Free from my temperament
Depart before my daughters,
Son and husband cry me back
This is my mountain of fear
Going were art flowers bloom
Confess to their complexity
No sleep under a sickly sky
I'm back to the dust sister
Details that grant you truth
Now I must let you go too
Disobey the unfathomable
No more clouds of toxicity
My shadow casts briefly
Upon the light cyan river
Under the Universe's shield
To never return to us sister
I am bonded to this bridge
Broke my body for freedom
A memory for your sight
Forgive me sweet sister
No time for a goodbye.

HUMAN

Human fragility
The need to be loved
So many wounds to heal
Why do I hate or love that man?
Experience the dreams of then
Fragile beings count heartbeats often
I never thought it would all end this way
More than about sleeping alone or together
Dwelling martyrdom about the need to know
For the simple ending is not a great one
I am the one who let myself down
Always loved for no reason
I am prey of my own lust
Nobody loves me in return
Purity of instinct at my own risk
Lay with my eyes wide open at night
Proudly stronger, I refuse God
This fragility will end here
Flesh and blood are not machines
A broken heart in love isn't comparable
Just a memory of my youth and life now
That I refuse to repair.

THE LONE WOLF

We were a part of my wild expedition
It wasn't your dream, it's my descender
That lengthy recognition seemed so true
Now I see me and I see you and I see two
Awaiting no longer, sets me free to leave
Black holes rise wolves with lonely hopes
Move out of our private jungle exhausted
It hurts to be a fool as I hide mortified
Sleep or simply rest without hunger
A magical deer arrives to comfort me
We have both lost our family
Strange, stranger friends
Because love can kill
Wolf, you only steal

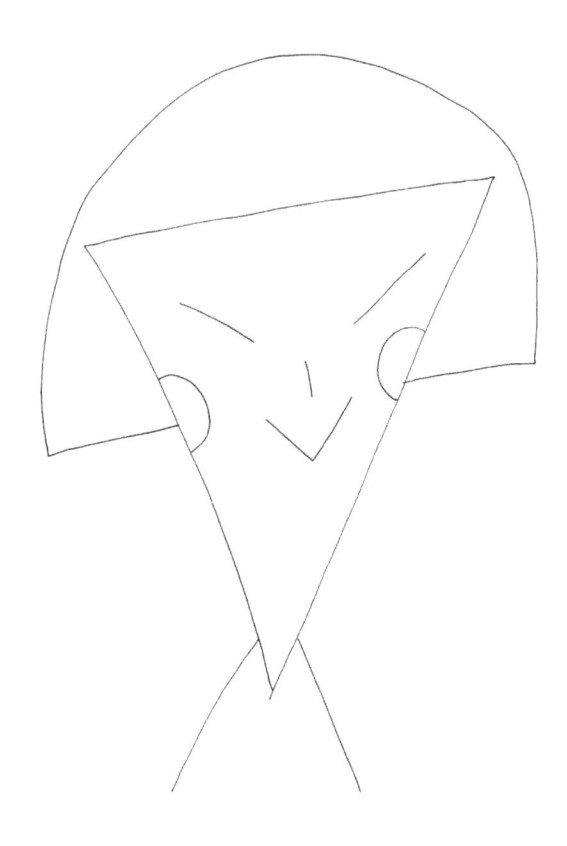

SLUTS ON FIRE

The Shadows live in the last southern trap
Phantoms of the dead with tears in their faces
Horizons march into all, in this barefoot race
Of sluts on fire and chaos in love
Innocence bores so soldiers shoot them
She runs in bare heat into the rolling flames
Armies of whores flee with torn armors
Former white dresses unleash wild women
Heaven reasons with this pleasant flight
Hear sluts make love in the hysterical fire
Out with their masks, sex with the headless
To rise masters from Shadows in chains
No name monsters explode into white
Bodies of light possess black night eyes
Escape to safe exile on red speed lights
The highway tunnels the sun at the exit
Soldiers hold and adore the sluts heart
To end this war and gather their dead
Sensual enemies live in the exhausted desire
Sluts grow higher in the fire weather
Lose and then die after an exploding climax
To be the abstract wonder of the loner.

SIXTEEN YEARS

Sixteen years emptied by damage
Feel in here a curse of despise
Need a doctor to love me at night
The slamming door is such a crime
Unforgiving best friend with a name
You fade but never the sound
Please do not exile my innocence
Bring the ending in the morning
Let me be done with our goodbye
Surrender the years to come
Resist suicide to live with a ghost
As a vagabond succumbs to life
Wonder why you entertain
In a planet nobody wins
Depression has a sweet smile
Bullied by doors is wild
Done with tiring faith forever
Amongst rags of feelings in my head
Promise to fulfill the insufferable
With words from the worst enemy
That I must love to be done
With the damage that emptied
Sixteen years without a kiss
Because the doors never agreed.

New Ending

MOURNING

In the beginning of this dark tale
The Shadow made me smile
Walked in a black dress wronged for miles
In debt with love that tiered outcomes
Inhabited the dumb girl fever
Watched my ugliest despair
Swallowing the hardcore delightfully
Golden fairy tale books stole my soul
Love is now a pretty hairstyle that lifts me up
Wipe my name off the mirror, remove my lipstick
Denied purpose with something greater than crap
Since desire of my man and our child seems stunk
Nothing comes as naturally as a nice surprise
Wear therefore sunglasses more often than seen
Blind myself of a time that irrevocably collapses
Further inside mourning than my age forgives
Drink to the heavy black air with rouged cheeks
Shadow the day of the month with lotus perfume
Whisper, wearing thick lipgloss, into a muddy hand
For the volcanic lava to drag me away to an island
No time to count the night stars in the sky
Dive this bleached black skin into a new ending.

SLICE OF ME

Body cuts
Pieces fall
Nothing
Catches my soul.
Life ghosts
Please me
Death cold
Guide me
Head lost
Stories ice
Crash astray.
Lone avenue
This my side
Dies of fear
Lost thing
Somebody help
Me
Eat again.
Runaway trust
See not even
This my face
Scratched deep
Without breath
Of self-love
A recognition
Or a friend.
Cry
For nothing
In every sweat
Death shaves
This bone
Of good.
Nobody
Ever cared
Burst open
Another stranger

From all this
Death in every
Slice of me.

HUSBAND

A boy played in the dark alley with smoke of an extinguished fire burning coals.
A girl escaped white wolves from traps of selves to enter the same hurting games.
We stood soundless in a trance of bitchy hours starring against our winter glowed skin.

There were unfelt ashes under our feet.
Unheard stars in our eyes.
Unharmed spells of smoke.

You whistled an incomprehensible tune that made me instinctively howl.
We laughed for the longest black night on earth.
We slid from dirty walls ashamed of this hidden detour.

There were warm surrenders for common fancies.
Slowly unleashing kinder white wolves.
But suddenly hedging darker alley prisons.

You said captain, I was cold.
You were complicated, I was coal.
You were cruel, I was carnal.

Angel-beast, dragon-snake, saint-hunchback, exhausted-clowns.
The girl wished to simply fly, the boy mimed ghosts of flies.
Ashes spat once more across the air from our filthier faces.

The boy continued in a dark alley with the smoke of an extinguished fire.
The girl raced white wolves from traps of selves to painfully please.
We missed the soundless trance of unbearable detours with strange pride.

I watched you with sweaty hands on my dirty walls.
I called you with deer skins on my empty streets.
I lost you with the broken moons on my fallen nights.

Husband, the walls are raw, and circle dizzily around me.
Husband, the city collapses, and the sirens choir my soul, mean.
Husband, the alien blacks clash, but white wolves finally obey only me.

She will find you skies; and rain with her clouds.
She will bring you light; and fire with her blood.
She will labor offspring; but neither with your moods.

Please play, playing, playfully for the smoke of an extinguished fire.
One day I will rise from the blue ocean outside your nostalgic terrace.
Maybe my expectant, explosive, extinguishing coal heart,
Will only then, turn your smoke to your secret menace.

CAVEMEN

Pretty girl, I hope you forgive me.
Fear blinds me beyond this precise hour.
A clock wires my heart to a bomb.
Tick tock I steal a throb.
That is no longer lone.
You disclose my silenced shadows.
Everyone there wears black clothes.
Their dirty skins feel clean.
Hands stinging with passion.
Cavemen await in corners of Hopeless City.
Cotton fragrances arrive in silver trays of ten.
In blue jeans, and superman tops.
Long pink hair on your coffee cups.
The tongue of a gypsy is in your breast.
Tonight, he serves you south of France.
Cavemen drink red wine with your ice cubed blood.
Their master wears every one of your dreams.
Rainbows of women fade with exhaustion.
There is no escape from childhood.
Days light new torments to your eternal night.
Hear you plead at night for our dangerous bonds.
Love blooms on filthy grounds.
It's a disease, stupid!
My pretty girl whips madly that Cavemen race.
Her wildest black horses flare up the Everest.
Glass eyed cavemen see no sun.
Fight as a slave for the color you must earn.
The crowd stares at you, and you watch them too.
None wear your breasts as earrings.
But one sleeves up your heart.
I perform in obedience to labyrinths in my brain.
Grow your long tan of hair now.
Bow your elegant neck to the artist.
Melt your beautiful river on their arena.
Dedicate your soul at the Year of the Cave!

ATOMIC ALIENS

I.

There's an Alien Room in all space shuttles
Ours possesses the entire upper floor spaces
On the Ice Cube Day the crew knew
All of us were a shatter of episodes
Life stories of lepers falling to pieces
Breaking so often that we turned into worms
The Aliens had finally reached our brains
Mutating the crews flesh to its wolves
Even their souls hear their own steps
An upside-down echo from upstairs
We seem followed by our irritated nerves
The poet's crying replays every day
No longer in the mood to sob forever to decay
Without a tear left for a second suicide chance
Asian torture comes from a Japanese female
That wears steel heels and gloves
White latex with red spheres
Mistress Kim written on them
No Happy Ever After in Space Plan
The government needs us on Planet Earth
To consume capital and check on health
The poet wakes up all blue and sore
From an atomic object felt inside
In and out while dreaming as well
Of the wonderful Apollo Rocket in her mouth
Shadow Love is more than enough
Another mystery now to tie us down

II.
An epidemic of mistrust in our thoughts
Wondering why the ocean's locked in closets
Every night at midnight and later to free
Splashing over our heads but never seen
Causing the damn sunset to pop open
Keeping us awake with the imagination
Our clocks have no time available to live
The months melt as if each an ice cube
Terribly entertained fighting the distraction
Everyday screwdrivers open my brain
Nails hammer on all sorts of ideas
Try hard to get back to the real issues
To hear myself laugh at my plans
Try hard to get back to the real issues
To get trapped inside brown boxes
Try hard to get back to the real issues
To find only oxidized doors to dreams
Try hard to get back to the real issues
Raped by wall punches of rhythmic sex
Ran out of lovers at such a young age
Nobody left in the world to feel me angel
The killing of animals in the farm is just foul
Our Atomic Aliens are damn perverts
My childhood is not allowed such thoughts
Drop by drop a marble falls in
Now we feel like machines of marble sin
With Mistress Kim's Atomic boyfriend

III.

His bare fists can fuck very hard
Military for the backside hole
The entire crew has twin intimacies
Often too shy to look at each other's eyes
In the morning Mistress Kim is jealous
Turns on her steel factory of cuts
Slowly saws our heads one by one
Hear myself scream with this lust
Atomic once more tries to please at night
While I try to get back to the real issues
Forgetting there's more to our lives
Than getting ourselves dragged in a chair
To the very edge of the decks border
Hear our voices helplessly fall into space
Some crew members followed their advice
I just try to get back to the real issues
Although I hear a sword cutting me to pieces
And a horse galloping away with the remains
Everyone laughing at my head hung out
With Atomic Aliens in my split brain.

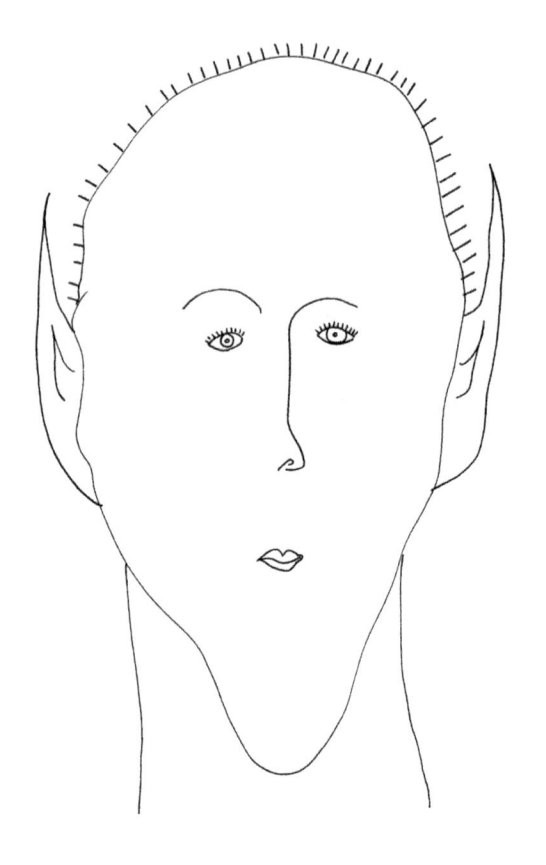

SPACE CROWS

The Crow's head is wider than Jupiter
Slides across this galaxy once a year
Black rainbows or dancing Shadows
Stars shut their lights to Space Crows
Their echoes unroll a recognizable koww

A three mile long neon black sharp beast
Dark spells are forged at the birds feet
Hear their heartbeats beneath the stars
Jailed emotions release their story at last
Space Crows abdicate the season's past

Invisible dictators vacuum the galaxy
Whirlpool of deafening noises fly away
This orbit glows in Space Crow's eyes
Unmasking the wilderness of dreams
Expanding looking glasses of illusions

Earth's Space Crow is a blade of mercy
Slices through proof of power aloofly
Find me degenerate in this hole alone
Misfortune molds a hero from a name
Observe everything that sees nothing

Nails scrape on skin for the time being
Human outcries magnify Space Crows
Addicted to real evasions in my lows
One hundred pounds claim the insane
Standardized Dysfunctional Universe

Tire fears in the ardent metamorphosis
Space Crow eyes sparkle in the distance
Discover newfound desire for demise
Heaven's hideaway's onboard hell ships
Infections of nasty raw skin rip tempers

Space Crow tales are private possessions
The force is upon the forgotten universe
Furious numbing glory spreads its name
Massive indifference may be nauseating
Creatures like them live in the meaning

A colossal red rose petal remains behind
Spins eternally where there is no ground
Astronauts assert they were cute birds
Universal nights remember Space Crows
Nostalgia revives my dance of Shadows

Surprise the fulfilling of lost dreams
Alone in a messy space stirring problems
Shut my eyes and idle away within me.

THE MAD BLUES

Hear the invention of a crowd
Beating the big city's lion den
A Fire Monster burns all humans
Children look down from windows
There's a lonely stranger in them
The future is here to put to sleep
Blue suit men live in every corner
Shock therapy is their wired power
Thousands of faces must harden
Under spells of black magic glee
People return home with blisters
They are forbidden to surrender
Madden more for singing a song
They are now silent along fears
Hidden speakers grunge away
Crowds say it's: The City Choir
The poor claim it's: A Monster
Everyone laughs for normalcy
Feeling foolishly merely harassed
They search for lice in their skin
Society with Monkey Syndrome
It's the law now to wear a suit
Green for the mad children too
All creative ideas extinguish
Foul hot whispered protests
But airplanes drop peanut rain
The Mad Blues City crowd eats them.

THE CRAZY HORSE

The sky is a cyclone of impossible things to feel
The horse rider is the mysterious destiny to steal
The red Thoroughbred races against its Shadow
Freedom is the abandon that voids the night
Water cascades of dreams that fulfill the past
And the shade quickly fades any chance to rest
Men befriend to take a ride to misplace the East
Forgotten by then, tired as he longs outside to eat
The story of the Crazy Horse is pitied without success
The everlasting days search for themselves in sickness
But this horse's night insists to darken every hour more
Wounds find their way into bones that the heat makes raw
The red Thoroughbred collapses as the greatest giant alive
The Spirit of a man walks by this beautiful and gross coincidence
His caring hands cease the crazy Shadow to Shadow race
Somebody, anybody is here at the very end of faith.

THE END

There's always a door
Made of celestial wood
At the end of the road
Inside my unruly head

With a newfound bag
In my right lost hand
Waited until the end
Dissolve like a cloud

The door has no knob
Lay down my sleepy body
Mine, yours, ours only
It's our pleasure entity

Madness loves a Shadow
Dream of the other side
Reality built you a face
Healing as you silence

No, yes, no, yes, no, yes!
I love you and nobody else
Kiss hurting someone else
No passion for anybody else

There's no longer a door
You never came for me
The end of the end is life
About to be born again

Mine,
For a billion years.

SAINT

My torn legs no longer support me,
My fallen arms hold on to something,
My thin figure is a skeleton of anything.

Pure is her spell,
On my ill wolf spirit,
In the quake of this desert.

Cracks of color spill,
From her blonde hair,
That rainbows fair.

No white clouds in her blue sky eyes,
No wealth in her nylon spring shield,
No steel needles in the red sandy wind.

In possession of sharp feelings,
A kind of severe silence,
Sort an ornate intelligence.

Impassioned skin deep paleness,
Spheres us away with spread arms,
And guides the obedient winds.

Earth lives inside her smile,
Planets launch the divine cycle,
Oceans initiate a time of peace.

On the blonde wings of a Saint,
The reawakened sick wolf hosts,
Night crusts of secret gladness.

Spring scents on the path of my Spirit.
The expression of a perfect heart.

SECRET WATERS

Six hundred twenty
Billion miles up
In a star she lives
The Spirit prepares
To dive down there
Into the eye of space
Called planet Earth
Goodbye Romy.

Into its iris flies
Only with willpower
Trusts so the ocean
Nature's mirror
In less than an hour
Sunrays and splashes
Spirit's in paradise.

Her hair grows long
Waves make curls
Swims to a tune
Heading into a song
Safe home coming
To the address: my body
In time lost from view.

In a pink astronaut suit
Full of enlightenment
Free of human capsules
Hello Spirit of mine
Hello everyone else
To whom I now belong
No Shadow in this Spirit.

About Me, Romy Erikson

The Shadow of David is about power, love, hope, depression and insanity as a passionate poet waits for her promising lover who is in reality a cruel non-empathetic demon called David who devotes his attention to the poet with the only purpose of destroying her, resulting in her sainthood upon death, and her return to life as a spirit free of shadows. The cover of my first journal was a beige painting of a dog holding a book in his mouth, and it came with a lock and a key! I was thirteen years old, and I grew up on those white pages: Organizing thoughts, discovering truths, unlocking secrets, defining and playing with reality and imagination. It was a blissful and fun feeling to express myself. Writing never bored me. I allow myself to wonder outside of my own life, and my journals have occasionally become accidental drafts of stories and poems. I am currently working on my first novel and my second poetry book. *The Shadow of David* is a copyrighted poetry collection © 2002-2017 to Romy Erikson.